Stowaway to California!

Adventures

with Father
Junipero Serra

By   Natalie Nelson Hernandez

Illustrations by Claudia Nolan

Stowaway to California
Adventures with
Father Junipero Serra
by
Natalie Nelson Hernandez

Author's Preface

This is a work of fiction based on true facts from Father Serra's life. The characters of Ramon, Pedro and others are imaginary. There really was an Indian boy named Jose Maria who went with Father Serra and was killed by Indians in San Diego. Little is known of Father Serra's early life. The events listed here of his boyhood are fictitious.

Also by Natalie Nelson-Hernandez:

"Mapmakers of the Western Trails, Adventures with John Charles Fremont"

"Stowaway to California" Available in Spanish under the name "Adventuras con Padre Serra"

"Captain Sutter's Fort" A work of fiction based on the life of John August Sutter (Coming fall 1997)

ISBN 09644386-0-7

Printed in the U.S.A.
First printing, December 1994
Second printing, September 1997

Table of Contents

This image is reproduced by permission of The Huntington Library,
1151 Oxford Road, San Marino, California 91108 (818) 405-2175

Chapter 1

The Lost Dog

"Hey, there, little Miguel. You are as weak as a mouse. All you do is sit in the house. Come on and break rocks with us and plow the ground like we do," shouted a group of boys.

Walking home from school Miguel José Serra was so deep in thought that he scarcely heard the boys taunting him. He remembered the stories that the priest told about kind, gentle St. Francis who loved animals. St. Francis founded the Franciscan order of priests in the Catholic church and Miguel dreamed of joining the Franciscans when he reached his 15th birthday.

After school the boys usually gathered around Miguel to listen to him tell stories. They liked him because of his intelligence and because he never refused to help others. Even though he was small and often sick he still found lost calves and lambs better than the others because he never stopped looking.

However, today the boys felt like making mischief and began teasing Miguel. One boy pushed Miguel and laughed. Miguel got up as the boys went running down the road. He tried to keep up but fell behind and had to stop to catch his breath. Only his feelings were hurt as his face turned red with anger.

"Come and catch us," they taunted as they came back and circled around him.

Miguel lost his temper when the others bullied him and he pushed a bigger boy. Outnumbered he swung his small arms and clenched fists. He landed a few punches, but they soon over-powered him. Two boys held him down while the others continued to tease him.

At that moment, Ramón, a big, strong boy,

came up the narrow dusty path. His black eyes shone with anger when he saw his friend on the ground. He pulled the boys off Miguel and slapped and scolded them.

"Pick on someone your own size," he snapped as he pummeled them.

"He hit us first," whimpered one boy whose nose was bleeding.

"I find that hard to believe," said Ramón, "I'll bet you were teasing him."

Miguel's mouth was bleeding and he had a cut over one eye. The boys all ran off then. They were afraid of Ramón, and also they were beginning to regret what they had done. They really liked Miguel and hadn't meant to hurt him.

"Come along with me, Miguel. Don't let those foolish boys bother you."

"Thank you, Ramón, I appreciate your help, but I can fight my own battles. Let's go down to the beach and I'll wash off in the sea. I don't want my mother to see me bleeding."

The boys lived in the small town of Petra on the island of Majorca in the Mediterranean Sea near Spain. After a swim Miguel and Ramón walked home.

When they arrived at Miguel's house Miguel said, "Goodbye and thanks again, Ramón. I'll see you at school next week."

A few days later Miguel heard Ramón's voice outside his window.

"Come out and play, Miguel," Ramón called from in front of the Serra's little house.

"Oh, no, thanks, I would rather read," answered Miguel looking out the window.

"Come on, it's a beautiful day and there's no school. I have my donkey and dog. Get your donkey and we can ride along the beach by the

4

cliffs," coaxed Ramón.

"All right, Ramón, let's go," agreed Miguel.

Ramón ran his fingers through his dark curly hair. Miguel had straight black hair and brown eyes. Ramón towered over his short friend.

The boys rode their donkeys along the beach close to the high cliffs overlooking the beautiful blue Mediterranean Sea. They saw many limestone caves along the way. Suddenly Ramón's dog ran up a path cut into the nearby cliff and disappeared from sight.

"Blanco," shouted Ramón, "Come back. Where are you?"

"I think I saw him run up the path to that ledge on the cliff," said Miguel. "Let's go look for him."

"Blanco, Blanco", called Ramón. The two boys heard an answering bark from half way up the cliff. The cliff was steep, but the wind and rain continuously carved paths, ledges and caves from its soft limestone face.

"Blanco," shouted Ramón again.

They heard a faint bark. Ramón and Miguel climbed carefully up toward the spot

5

from which they thought they heard the dog. The rocks below made them realize the danger of falling. The limestone crumbled under their sandals and sent pebbles raining down to the beach like miniature avalanches. When they reached the ledge, Ramón called again and they realized that Blanco had entered one of the numerous caves that could be found on the cliffs. Looking into the small cave they heard Blanco scratching.

"Should we go in after him?" asked Ramón.

"I don't think so," said Miguel. "We have no torch, and it's dark in there. The opening is very narrow. Also no one knows we have come here. Call him again and maybe he will come out."

"Blanco, come here," called Ramón.

The boys heard an answering bark and then a pitiful whining and scratching sound.

"Maybe he's hurt or caught and can't get out," said Ramón.

"I'll go in after him,' said Miguel. "I'm small and able to crawl through narrow spaces."

"Are you sure you want to do this?" asked Ramón. "You might slip and be unable to get out yourself."

"I'll be careful, and anyway you can go for help if anything happens."

The boys heard the dog whining and scratching as though he were trying to return to his master. Miguel squeezed cautiously through the narrow opening. He found that he had to be on his hands and knees on the floor of the cave as it wasn't high enough for him to stand up. He waited for a moment for his eyes to adjust to the dimness inside the cave.

"Are you all right?" called Ramón from outside anxiously.

"Yes," answered Miguel, "I'm letting my eyes get used to the darkness."

"Can you see Blanco?" asked Ramón.

"Yes, and he did get stuck trying to go through another opening. I'll try to help him out."

Blanco whined again as Miguel crawled close to him. Miguel realized that only the dog's hindquarters were on his side. He grabbed the dog's hind legs and tried to pull him back. Blanco yelped in pain so Miguel stopped pulling and then tried to scratch away the soft limestone from around Blanco's body. It was slow work but Miguel managed to widen the opening and then gently pulled again on Blanco's legs.

Little by little, by pulling on the dog's legs and digging the crumbling stone away, Miguel managed to free the frightened dog. Miguel shouted to Ramón to call his dog, and Blanco scampered back out of the cave when he heard his master's voice.

Just then the limestone crumbled under Miguel's feet. He fell through and landed on the floor of another cave below him. Miguel let out a shout as he fell. He was stunned as he hit the hard floor. As his senses returned he realized that he wasn't hurt, but now how to get out? He couldn't reach the opening over his head, and the walls were smooth and straight.

"What happened?" yelled Ramón. "Where are you? Why don't you come out?"

"I fell into another cave," shouted Miguel. "It's very dark in here and I don't know if I can climb out."

"I'll go for help," said Ramón.

"No, wait and I'll see if I can scramble out somehow."

Miguel tried to find a handhold or foothold on the side of the cave but soon found out that the sides were too steep and too crumbling for him to climb up.

"Okay, Ramón, you will have to get help. Be sure to bring a torch and a rope. Get Jaime and Antonio to help and maybe you won't have to tell my parents."

Miguel sat down on the floor of the cave to wait. He heard his friend tell Blanco to stay by the hole. Then he heard Ramón's footsteps fading away. The time passed slowly and it seemed like a long time while he waited there in the dark, so he began to pray as the priests had taught him. Finally he heard voices and Blanco barking.

"Here, over here," he shouted.

"I'm back," yelled Ramón. "Here are Jaime and Antonio." Ramón stuck his head in the hole and then thrust the torch inside.

"Don't come in," called Miguel. "You might fall in here with me. Just throw in the rope. Can you see the place where I fell?"

"Yes," answered Ramón as he stuck the blazing torch into the cave.

"Fasten a stick or stone to the end of the rope and then throw it down through the hole," suggested Miguel.

"All right," agreed Ramón.

Miguel heard a clunk as the rock hit right beside his foot on the floor of the small cave.

I'm glad it didn't hit me on the head, he thought, as he felt around for the rope.

"I've got it," he shouted and tied the rope around his body under his arms. "Can you pull me up?"

The three boys tugged hard on the rope and Miguel tried to scrabble up with his hands and feet on the side of the cave as they pulled him out. It hurt as the rough stone scraped his skin.

"What a narrow escape," said Ramón. "Our father in heaven must have been looking out for you."

"I did say some prayers," said Miguel.

"Are you okay?" asked Ramón.

"Yes," answered Miguel. "How is Blanco?"

"He has some scratches, a lame leg, and a sore paw, but otherwise he's all right."

"My hands are sore and scratched, too," said Miguel. "I'm glad to get out of there and I'm glad that Blanco is okay."

"Let's go for a swim in the sea. We are all sweaty and you, Miguel, are covered with dust. We can wash off Blanco, too. The salt water will be good for his scratches."

After splashing and swimming to refresh themselves, the four boys returned to the village and agreed not to tell anyone of their adventure.

"Our parents would only worry and forbid us to come here again," said Miguel.

Chapter 2

The Fishing Trip

The next day Miguel woke up early and every bone and muscle ached from his ordeal and pain of the day before. But he got up and got dressed to get ready to help on the farm. He was often sick so his mother said, "Be sure to eat a good breakfast and dress warmly before you go out."

"Oh, Mother," answered Miguel, "it's summer and nice and warm out. I'll take the sheep and cows out on the hillside to graze."

Miguel's father, a stonecutter, was getting ready to leave for the quarry where he worked cutting marble all day.

"I wish I could go and help you, Father,"

said Miguel.

"Take care of the livestock, Miguel, and study hard at school. That's how you can help me," answered his father.

Miguel drove the animals out of their pen. As he rode the old donkey, he met Ramón on his donkey and the two friends continued on to the pasture.

"One of my father's cows is lost and I must find her," said Ramón.

"I'll help you," said Miguel.

The boys began to ride up the steep hillside. They left the Serra's animals in the pasture to eat grass. They looked back down on the valley and saw the neat rows of grapevines in the vineyards and smelled the sweet scent of the orange blossoms. The almond trees were no longer blooming and now had lovely green leaves. They could see the small town of Petra and the orange tile roofs of the houses.

"Where can that cow be?" asked Ramón. "We looked yesterday for her."

"We'll find her," said Miguel. "Let's look up in that ravine and in the pine grove.

"Everyone says that you never give up looking for a lost animal, Miguel, even when the other searchers are worn out," remarked Ramón.

"Remember the story about the lost sheep in the Bible?" answered Miguel. "I think about that when I'm looking for lost animals. Also I want to be like St. Francis. He loved all animals."

The boys searched and searched. Finally they heard the sounds of an unhappy cow. "I think it came from behind those trees," said Miguel.

"You're right," answered Ramón. "Let's get off and walk over there to see."

The boys tied their donkeys to a tree and began to walk quietly in the direction from which they had heard the noise. Suddenly a large bull with huge horns came thrashing out of the bushes toward them.

"Run!" shouted Ramón.

"Climb a tree!" exclaimed Miguel.

The boys scrambled quickly up the nearest tree as the enraged bull charged furiously at them. The bull glared up at them in frustration and bellowed loudly.

"That must be Garcia's bull from the next farm," stated Ramón. "Maybe that's why our cow ran off."

After awhile the bull became bored and wandered off. The boys slid down the tree. They cautiously walked toward the spot where they had heard the cow. They found her standing by some bushes. They drove her back to their donkeys, keeping a careful lookout for the bull. They went back down the mountain to the pasture where the other animals were grazing.

"I see some fishing boats coming in to the harbor," said Ramón.

"Yes, they're coming to dock at the wharf," said Miguel. "Let's go and talk to the fishermen. Maybe they'll take us out with them on their next trip."

"Will your mother let you go?" asked Ramón. "You get sick so easily."

"She might if I promise to wear my father's wool coat. Mother always has me up and back to work even if I do get sick often. She helps me ignore my sickness," answered Miguel.

They came back to where they had left the Serra's animals and herded them with Ramón's cow back to the village and put them in their pens.

"Now let's go talk to the fishermen," said Miguel.

"Okay, let's go," agreed Ramón.

As the boys came near the wharf they saw

17

the men unloading their catch of fish. The boys helped them finish up, and then sat on the pier and listened to them talk. The seamen told stories of the far off lands of China and the Indies. They talked of Peru and Mexico in the New World which was also called New Spain. The sailors told about the strange wild Indians there. Miguel and Ramón were interested in Mexico and California most of all.

"When are you going out to fish again?" Miguel asked.

"Probably with the tide this evening and then return sometime tomorrow with the fish," answered one fisherman.

"Can we go with you?" asked Ramón.

"Certainly," answered the captain. "You can help us. Just go and get permission from your parents."

The boys ran off and begged their parents to let them go.

"Just this once," said Miguel's mother, "since it's a warm evening. But wear your warmest clothes anyway and try not to get wet."

Pulling on his jacket Miguel ran back to the

wharf. He shouted out to Ramón that he could go.

Ramón called back, "My father said that since we found the cow, this is our reward."

They jumped into the boat. The men raised the sails and they slowly left the wharf. They moved out into the Mediterranean Sea away from Petra.

"This is great," said Ramón.

"Stay out of the way for now," said the captain. "We'll let you know what you can do and how you can help us later."

Excitedly Ramón and Miguel watched the coastline recede until the island was no longer in sight. The waters of the Mediterranean reflected the beautiful clear blue of the sky above and seagulls white as snow wheeled over the boys as they looked for fish.

The sailors prepared the nets and and uncovered the openings to the hold that smelled of the fish that had previously been unloaded.

"There is a school of fish!" shouted one seaman.

"Get ready to cast off the nets," ordered the

captain.

Fascinated by all the activity the two boys stayed close to the railing to keep out of the way and also to have a good view of the work. Miguel José leaned over the rail to see the fish and watch how the men threw the net.

"Don't lean over too far," warned Ramón, "You might fall in."

"Oh, don't worry," replied Miguel loftily, "I'm a good swimmer."

Just then the boat dipped over low into the water as the nets filled with fish and pulled the boat over with their weight. Suddenly Miguel lost his grip on the railing. He fell into the sea and went down, down, down. After what seemed like an eternity, he surfaced gasping for air. Salt water stung his eyes and throat.

"Help!" yelled Ramón, "Miguel fell into the water."

"Man overboard," shouted a seaman, as Ramón stood paralyzed with shock and fear.

Quickly the men threw a line to the frightened boy who struggled frantically in the water. Miguel tried to tread water to keep his head above the waves. He grabbed the rope and

started to swim back toward the boat. Suddenly he felt something wrap around his legs. His heart hammered in his chest. Was it a shark or a sea monster?

"Something's got me," he cried. "It's pulling me under."

"I think it's the net," said the captain, "Pull the boy and the net together into the boat.

Everyone worked hard to lift the boy with the net full of fish. As the net and boy came over the side, the men dumped Miguel uncere-

moniously into the hold with the catch of fish.

"Are you hurt?" shouted Ramón anxiously.

"No," sputtered Miguel as he scrambled around among the slippery fish. "Ugh, what a smell."

Ramón helped him climb up out of the hold. "You're right, Miguel," he said, holding his nose. "You're a mess."

"Let's throw him back in," laughed one of the seamen.

"Here is a bucket of water to clean yourself. Next time don't lean so far over the rail and be sure to hang on when the boat tips," said the captain.

Another seaman brought some dry clothes and Miguel washed himself off and put them on. Ramón dunked the wet clothes into the bucket and hung them up to dry.

"It's a good thing that the weather is warm, Miguel"

"Don't tell my mother about this, Ramón. She will never let me come again."

"I may not allow it either," said the captain crossly. "You have delayed our fishing and our catch is small because of having to stop to rescue you. Also I would never forgive myself if something worse had happened. I would have had to tell my good friends, your father and mother, about your accident."

"I promise I will be more careful," said Miguel.

The next day when Miguel returned home, his mother noticed that his clothes were stiff and smelled strongly of fish.

"What happened, son?" she asked.

"Oh, not much, Mother," answered Miguel. He couldn't lie to her and he hoped that she would not keep asking about the trip. To stop her questions he told her about the fishing trip and the fish the men had caught.

"The waves came over the side and we got wet, Mother," he said. "Also when the nets filled with fish, the heavy catch pulled the boat over close to the water."

His mother just smiled and went on with her chores. Exhausted Miguel went to bed early.

Chapter 3

Life in Petra

The next day Miguel came down with a fever and stayed in bed. His mother took good care of him. During his previous illnesses she helped him to bear the pain and discomfort without complaining. She encouraged him to get up and get back to his regular duties as soon as possible after being sick.

After Miguel recovered, he and Ramón walked to school together. They liked to listen to the priests' stories about America and the Indians who lived there. The priests told even more interesting facts than the sailors.

"The California Indians wear no clothes because it's always warm. It's much like here in Majorca. People used to think California was an island, too. California is near the Pacific Ocean as Majorca is in the Mediterranean Sea. California Indians eat only nuts and berries and they live in grass huts. The Indians cannot read or write. They have no books and do not know about God. There are no churches."

The boys hung on every word. Miguel felt sorry for the poor Indians and wished to help them. He dreamed of going to the New World to convert the Indians and teach them the Christian faith. Miguel wanted very much to be a priest.

One day Miguel went to Ramón's house. "It's time to go to school, Ramón."

"I'm not going to go much longer," said Ramón.

"Why not?" asked Miguel. "There's so much to learn and the fathers work hard to teach us."

"I know," said Ramón, "but school is hard for me and I've learned to read a little and do some arithmetic. I am a farmer and I don't need to learn more. I'm 12 now, and my father needs me on the farm. Also I have a girlfriend and I want to get married some day."

"Sometimes I wish I were as big and strong and healthy as you are, but everyone is different," said Miguel. "I would like to be a farmer, too, as I like animals a lot, but I also like to read and study. I think I want to be a priest."

"Sometimes I wish I could read as well you. You are so smart," said Ramón. "How do you know so much?"

"I read a lot, study hard and I listen carefully to the fathers," answered Miguel.

"You must go on to school in Palma," said Ramón, "you have already learned everything the fathers here in Petra can teach you."

"Well, I would like to go," said Miguel. "I want to study to become a priest and I want to go to Mexico and California some day. Up to now only Cabrillo and Vizcaino have been to California. They say that California is a barren land with only savage Indians and wild animals living there. It's not good for anything. The explorers did not find gold there as they did in Mexico.

"Why do you want to go there then?" asked

Ramón.

"To teach the Indians and spread the word of God. I want to build missions and convert the Indians," answered Miguel Serra.

"What will you teach them?"

"First I will teach them about Jesus and Mary and the Bible. I will teach them how to farm and raise goats, chicken, sheep, and cattle like we do here in Majorca. They can learn to raise wheat, vegetables, and fruits. Then they will have plenty of food. Together we can build houses, weave cloth, and make clothes so they will not have to go naked and live in grass huts."

"How can you do this?" wondered Ramón.

"We'll take what we need with us. We'll take seeds, cuttings, and livestock."

"What if the Indians try to kill you?"

"We'll make friends with them, and anyway, they don't have guns."

"How will you talk to them?"

"I'll learn their language and teach them to speak Spanish as we do," answered Miguel.

"I want to go with you to Mexico and California to see these Indians," said Ramón.

"I'll be your helper. I'll take care of the live-stock for you and carry a gun to protect you. Perhaps I can be a soldier."

Miguel's little sister, Juana, came out from behind the bushes where she had been listening. "I want to go, too," she said.

"You can't go", said Miguel. "You're too little. It's too dangerous. We have to go across the ocean to Mexico and then travel across the country. It takes a long time and is very dangerous. Not very many women go."

"You are too small and weak to go, also. You should stay here and be a teacher," thought Ramón. But he didn't say it aloud because he didn't want to hurt his friend's feelings.

"I wonder what Mexico and California are like and if the Indians are as wild as the priest says. The voyage across the Atlantic Ocean is very long and uncomfortable. Many get sick. There are English pirates to worry about, too," said Ramón.

"Well, before I can even think of going to Mexico, I must go to Palma and study to become a priest. Then perhaps I can be a missionary. I hope to be a Franciscan father and follow the teachings of St. Francis," said Miguel.

Miguel José took Juana home and Ramón went to his home. There was no more talk of the going to the New World that day.

Chapter 4

Miguel becomes a Priest

Soon after his fifteenth birthday Miguel José applied to become a priest. Fifteen was the usual age to begin to study to be a priest. Being small for his age Miguel looked barely 13. Even when fully grown he only reached the height of five feet two inches. Miguel José went to see the Minister General, who was visiting in Petra, to ask permission to enter the priesthood. Miguel's nervousness almost made him stutter as he talked to the Minister General.

"I want to be a priest, sir," he said.

At first the Minister General spoke kindly to Miguel and said, "You must wait until you are

old enough. Come back when you are 15."

"But, sir, I am old enough. I'm 15 now and ready to apply," answered Miguel.

The Minister General became angry with him and accused him of lying. "You are too small to be 15. I think you are only 13 years old. A priest must never lie," he said.

Miguel felt a wave of heat rise within him and his face turned brick red. He never forgot how badly he felt when the Minister General did not believe him. Deeply hurt, he ran home and went off to the fields to be by himself and try to ease the awful feeling. It's terrible to be accused of lying when you're telling the truth.

Of course, later, the Petra priests talked to the Minister General and told him that Miguel really was fifteen. They said that Miguel always told the truth and that he was a very good student and should be accepted for the priesthood. They said that he was the best scholar they had ever had in Petra. In fact, they said, he has learned everything we have to teach here and should go to the university in Palma.

The Minister General apologized to Miguel for doubting him and happily accepted his application to study for the priesthood. Naturally Miguel forgave him, but he never forgot how terrible he had felt. Also he had been so worried that he might never become a priest.

Miguel's father and mother were very proud of him going to the university, but they were sad to see their son leave. The Serra family lived in poverty with little education. It was a great honor for Miguel José Serra to be chosen to study at the university at Palma, the capital city of Majorca.

The island of Majorca is sometimes spelled Mallorca. It is very similar to California in that it has fertile valleys as does California. Majorca's central valley is a rich agricultural area like the central valley of California. Pine trees and olive trees grow there. Majorca's farmers grow figs, apricots, oranges, almonds, grapes, and cereals. They raise cattle, sheep and goats. The climate is also much like California.

Miguel felt nervous about leaving his family and friends, but after he arrived at the university there was so much to learn and so many books to read that he was happy to be pursuing the career he wanted. He did miss Ramón and his other friends and his family but found two new close friends in Palma named Francisco Palou and Juan Crespi.

Miguel told them that his father had rushed him to the church on the day of his birth, November 24, 1713, so that he could be baptized immediately. His weakness made his parents fear that he would not live through the day. Miguel was the first of the Serra children to live. The other babies had all died shortly after birth.

Ramón stayed behind in Petra and helped his father on the farm. Later he married his girlfriend and began to raise a family. From time to time he heard news of Miguel from the priests and he still dreamed of going to the New World with him. After his marriage he named

his oldest son Miguel after his friend Miguel José. Ramón told his son about his friend. He talked of their dream of going to help the Indians of the New World. As Ramón's son listened to his father's stories, he began to dream of going there also.

Miguel José Serra became a priest in 1738 and took the name of Junipero because that was the name of a follower of St. Francis. Everyone called him Father Junipero Serra because he was now a priest. No one called him Miguel for the rest of his life.

Father Serra's hair was dark brown, thin and straight. After the fashion of the Franciscan priests he kept his head shaved with just a fringe of hair around the edges. He never did grow a beard. A short man, Father Serra always stayed thin and slight because he ate and slept very little and he worked very hard. After he recovered from his childhood illnesses he became strong and wiry. He wore the grey robe of the Franciscans with a knotted rope for a belt. He used simple sandals and around his neck he always hung a large cross even when sleeping.

Father Serra began teaching at the university. He talked to Father Crespi and Father Palou about his desire to go to Mexico and California to become a missionary. They also began to dream of going there with their friend and teacher, Father Serra.

The priests wanted Father Serra to stay at the university because he was such a good teacher and philosopher. He gave excellent sermons. They did not want him to go to Mexico.

Chapter 5

The Stowaway

One day Father Serra heard that a group of missionaries were leaving to go to Mexico. He applied for permission to go. Father Crespi and Father Palou also made out applications. At first they heard that the ship was full and they were not needed. Then they found out that three of the missionaries had changed their minds and decided not go. The three friends were overjoyed when they were chosen to take their places.

Father Serra went to Petra for a last visit. He wanted to see his mother and father for the last time. He didn't tell them where he was going because he didn't want them to worry.

He knew that he would probably never see them again. Then he went to say goodbye to his old friend, Ramón.

"I'm going to Mexico," Father Serra told him. "I have finally been accepted. I hope to go to California from there. My friends, Father Crespi and Father Palou, are going with me. We will sail next week."

Listening, Miguel saw the wistful look on his father's face. He knew his father still wanted to go, too. Later he asked, "Why don't you go, father?" (And take me with you, he thought to himself.)

"No, my son, I must stay here and take care of your mother and your sisters and brothers," answered Ramón sadly.

Miguel thought about this and said, "Father, if you can't go, I'll go in your place."

"Oh, no, Miguel, you are much too young for such a long dangerous voyage. Your mother would never forgive me if I let you go. Forget these foolish dreams that I had when I was a boy. Let Father Serra, Father Crespi, and Father Palou go. They will have men to help them. They don't need us."

Miguel thought to himself, "I'm not needed here in Petra. My father and mother have other sons. I'll go with Father Serra somehow."

He listened carefully to the men talking of the trip. First they would board a ship for Spain, then they take another ship to Veracruz, Mexico. Miguel went to the waterfront. He walked along looking for the name of the ship that he had heard Father Serra mention. Finally he found it. Later after dark he quietly climbed aboard and found a place to hide under some canvas in a lifeboat.

It was dark and uncomfortable in the little boat. He heard the noise of the passengers coming on board. Then he heard the shouts of the sailors and the anchor being lifted. After several days at sea Miguel felt hungry and cold. He was very much afraid of being discovered especially when he heard the captain's loud angry voice shouting at everyone. He lived in terror that the captain would throw him overboard if anyone found him.

Many times Miguel heard the captain shouting and arguing with the priests. He listened to Father Serra calmly answering the angry captain with logical arguments. They argued about religion. The priests belonged to the Catholic religion, but the captain belonged to the Church of England and he disagreed with the beliefs of the Catholic priests.

The captain sounded almost insane with anger because Father Serra answered all his arguments with reason. The captain was unable to convince him of his own logic. This made Miguel even more afraid than ever of revealing himself to be a stowaway.

One night the loud angry voice of the captain woke Miguel. However, this night he heard only the captain and Father Serra talking. The captain seemed almost berserk. Miguel peeped out from under the canvas and saw the captain attack Father Serra. It seemed to him that the captain was going to kill Father Serra. Miguel thought he saw a knife in the captain's hand. Father Serra fell senseless to the deck. The captain stomped off to his cabin with no regard for the fallen priest. Miguel was beside himself with fear; fear for himself, fear of the captain, but most of all, fear for Father Serra. Miguel crept out from under the canvas

and crawled silently and fearfully over to where the father lay motionless on the deck.

Miguel shook his shoulder gently, "Father, Father, are you all right?" he asked. Father Serra gasped for breath and tried to sit up.

"Who's there? Who is it?" he asked.

Miguel answered, "I am Miguel, the oldest son of Ramón. Here, let me help you."

"Thank you, my son, the captain was most brutal tonight. I fear that I lost consciousness from his attack."

"Let me help you to your cabin," said Miguel. "Here, lean on me and show me the

42

way."

Soon the boy and the priest arrived at the cabin door. "Let us in, Francisco," said Father Serra. "I am sorry, but I have met with a mishap and this boy helped me."

The door opened and Father Palou asked, "What happened, Junipero?"

"The captain became so angry that he attacked me," answered Father Serra.

"Oh, I should have been with you. I am so sorry," said Father Palou. "And who is this?"

"This is Miguel, son of my old friend, Ramón. He helped me get back to the cabin. Miguel, how is it that you are here? Are you part of the crew? I have not seen you before tonight."

"No, Father, I am a stowaway and very much afraid, especially of the captain."

"Oh, Miguel, you mean you ran away from home? What about your father and mother? They will be worried about you."

"I told my little brother to tell them after the ship had sailed," answered Miguel.

"Well, we will have to take care of this some-how," said Father Serra. "I thank you for helping me. But it was wrong to leave your father and mother without permission. It's also wrong to stow away on a ship and not pay for your passage."

"I'm afraid the captain will kill me or throw me overboard if he discovers me on his ship," said Miguel.

"That may be true," said Father Serra, "what shall we do?"

"He can hide in our cabin until we reach port," suggested Father Palou. "It won't be long until we dock. After what the captain did to you, we can't take a chance. Perhaps later we can send him money for Miguel's passage."

When they reached port of Malaga in Spain, the fathers helped Miguel sneak off the ship after dark. "Be sure to meet us at the church," said Father Serra. "I don't want you to get lost and get into more trouble in this city. I will write your parents that you are safe with me."

"My parents can't read, Father," said Miguel.

"Oh, yes, Ramón can read. Don't forget that he and I went to school together. Then must see about sending you back on the next ship."

"No, Father, please don't send me back. I want to go to Mexico and California with you. I will help you. My father always wanted to go with you, but now he cannot, so let me go in his place, please."

"That is true. Ramón did always want to go with me. I will think and pray about this, Miguel."

"He did help you already, Junipero," said Father Palou. "I think you owe him a debt of gratitude. He wants to go so badly and per- haps he could be useful."

Chapter 6

On to Mexico

A few days later they boarded the ship for Mexico. Miguel said, "Thank you, Father, for letting me come with you. You will never regret it. I'll work hard and help you in every way that I can."

"Please be careful, Miguel, and do not get into trouble. I feel responsible for you. It will be a long, uncomfortable voyage, I fear," said Father Serra.

After many weary days crossing the Atlantic Ocean, the food and water supplies began to get very low. "Why don't you talk much these days, Father?" asked Miguel. "Are you sick?"

"No, my son," answered Father Serra. "I

have found that if I do not talk, I feel less thirsty and less hungry. Try it."

The next day there was a terrible storm and the sailors and passengers were all very frightened. The wind blew hard and rain came down in sheets. Lightning flashed all around. The ship rocked back and forth like a baby's cradle. Frightened, Miguel stayed close to Father Serra. "Aren't you afraid, Father?" he asked.

"No, Miguel, I trust in our Father in Heaven." Father Serra suggested that everyone pray for deliverance. Soon the storm passed and they arrived in Veracruz, Mexico.

"Let us start out immediately for Mexico City," said Father Serra.

"Ah, yes, but how shall we get there?" asked Miguel.

"We shall walk, of course, as all good Franciscans do," answered Father Serra.

Miguel's heart sank as he would much rather travel through a strange land on muleback or horseback. He preferred to go in a caravan with wagonloads of supplies and soldiers to protect and guide them. I wonder how Father Serra will find the way he thought.

"Father Palou is too sick to walk with us. He will come later on horseback or in a wagon," said Father Serra. "You can wait and come with him, Miguel."

"No, no, Father, I will come with you," answered Miguel, although in his heart he would rather have waited.

Another priest named Father Perez came with them. The two priests and Miguel started off through the countryside to Mexico City with no supplies and no horses or mules. They had no map or guide. As usual Father Serra trusted in God to show them the way.

The hot weather made Miguel very hungry and thirsty. They traveled on a dusty trail and slept under bushes in the open air. One day they came to a wide river.

"How are we going to get across, Father?" asked Miguel.

"We must find a good place to ford," answered Father Serra.

As they traveled along the river looking for a place to cross, a man on horseback appeared on the other side.

"Where can we cross?" called Father Perez.

"Come along and I will show you," was the answer.

The three weary and hungry travelers followed on their side of the river. They finally came to a good crossing place. After they waded across the river, the horseman asked them where they were going.

"We are on our way to Mexico City," said Father Serra, "I wish to work in the missions with the Indians. I hope to go on to California some day."

"Come to my hacienda which is nearby," said the horseman. "You will have a good supper and a place to stay the night."

Miguel thought it was wonderful to eat a good meal at a table and sleep in a bed again. But the next morning Father Serra said that they must be off again. "Goodbye and thank you for your help," he said.

After several days of walking through the wild uninhabited country, the three travelers were exhausted and starving. Suddenly a hut appeared in the wilderness. A man, a woman, and a young boy stood in front of it and beckoned to them.

Miguel was frightened at the sudden appearance of the hut. He had been looking ahead and had seen nothing. Then he glanced away, and when he looked back, there was the hut. The people were dressed strangely and seemed not to have substance to them. It was

almost as if he could see through them. There seemed to be a glow around them as though light was shining from their bodies. They gave Miguel and the priests some food. Miguel was too exhausted to be uneasy or worry and they slept that night there.

The next day they left on their journey and met a group of mule drivers with a pack train. Father Serra told them of the hut in the desert.

The mule drivers said that there was no house in that place. Father Serra took them back to show them, but the hut had disappeared.

"Thanks be to God," said Father Serra, "we must have seen the Holy Family, Joseph, Mary and Jesus." Miguel shivered at the thought of spending the night with the Holy Spirits.

The muledrivers said that they were close to Mexico City and did not have far to go. The travelers started off again. Hordes of mosquitoes tormented them. Father Serra's legs swelled up from many mosquito bites. That night they slept under the stars. Suddenly Miguel awoke from a sound sleep. He thought he heard Father Serra cry out during the night. The next morning he noticed that the Father's leg was bleeding.

"What happened to your leg, Father?" Miguel asked.

"I don't know, my son," he answered. "Perhaps I scratched a mosquito bite and made it bleed."

"I thought I heard you cry out in the night," said Miguel.

"Let me look at it," said Father Perez, "I

wonder what caused this."

"Oh, it's just a mosquito bite," said Father Serra, "never mind about it."

"It might be a bite from a scorpion or a poisonous spider," said Miguel, "or maybe even a rattlesnake or a coral snake. Does it hurt?"

"Don't worry about it, Miguel," said Father Serra, "it doesn't matter."

As they walked along that day, Father Serra began limping more and more. That night he was feverish and his leg was swollen.

"You must see a doctor when we get to Mexico City," said Father Perez.

"We'll see," said Father Serra, "let's not talk about it."

Whatever bit Father Serra left him lame for life. The sore never healed properly and remained an open wound and pained him greatly. They never found out exactly what caused it. A later source speculated that it might have been the bite of a brown recluse spider. He limped for the rest of his life, even though he traveled from Mexico City to California and from mission to mission back and forth many times in California and almost always on foot.

Chapter 7

Trouble in Mexico City

Finally they arrived in Mexico City. Miguel had never seen such a large beautiful city. There was so much activity going on. He stared at the carriages and beautifully dressed ladies. They went to the monastery and the priests gave them food and a place to rest. Father Palou had already arrived and recovered from his illness. He worried about them and wondered why it had taken them so long to come. He noticed Father Serra's lame leg and tried to get him to see a doctor, but the father refused.

The next day Miguel accompanied Father Serra to the cathedral. On the way he became so interested in watching all the colorful Indians, the burros loaded with many strange things, the carriages of the rich people, and the soldiers that he became separated from Father Serra and was jostled away in the crowd. Suddenly a squad of soldiers came cantering along the narrow street. Miguel felt a hand grab his shoulder and pull him out of the way just in time or he would have been trampled under the horses' hoofs. While shaking in the doorway from his narrow escape, Miguel looked up to see a pair of black eyes in a reddish-brown face. The boy's straight hair was so black and shiny that it looked almost blue-black.

"You almost got it that time," said the tall Indian boy, "you have to be alert because the soldiers stop for no one except maybe the viceroy, the rich people, and the priests."

"Thank you," said Miguel. "Father Serra and I were on our way to the cathedral. Would you show me the way?"

"Yes," answered the Indian boy slyly. "My name is Rafael. What is your name?"

"I am Miguel and I have come from the

island of Majorca across the Atlantic Ocean with Father Serra. I'm going to go with him to California."

"I've heard of that," said Rafael. "Aren't you afraid to go so far from home? There's nothing in California except wild Indians."

"We're going there to teach the Indians to be Christians and to civilize them", answered Miguel. "I'm not afraid of anything when I'm with Father Serra."

"Well," said Rafael, "I work for the soldiers in the barracks. Our captain is Captain Rivera. He talks about California. Come with me. I will show you where the soldiers live."

"I should find Father Serra. He'll be worried about me."

"We have plenty of time," said Rafael. "You certainly have a nice jacket and boots."

Rafael led Miguel through many narrow, winding streets. Miguel completely lost his bearings and had no idea where he was. Suddenly a group of boys jumped out from a doorway and began hitting and kicking him. He tried to fight back, but there too many. He realized that Rafael was holding his arms to prevent him from defending himself. Before he lost consciousness he heard Rafael snarl, "His jacket and boots are mine. You can have the rest."

"Come on, let's carry him into the barracks."

Miguel heard a rough voice in the background as he slowly began to come to his senses. His head ached and he felt sore all over. He felt himself being lifted up roughly and carried into some dim room. He groaned as he was dropped on a rude cot and again lost consciousness. Later he thought he heard a voice in the distance.

"Well, he seems to be coming around," said the voice. "He must be one of the soldier helpers. Maybe he was trying to run away."

Miguel opened his eyes and saw a soldier with a black beard and moustache standing over him. "Where am I?" he groaned.

"You're okay," said the soldier. "You are in the barracks where you belong. You must be one of the junior privates. You weren't trying to run away from the army, were you?"

"I am not in the army," said Miguel. "Some boys attacked me and stole my clothes."

"That's funny, you are wearing the usual outfit of the soldier helpers."

Miguel looked down and saw that he was dressed in the clothes that Rafael had been wearing. "These are not my clothes," he said.

"Go get the corporal," the soldier ordered one of the boys who was standing around.

The corporal came in, highly irritated at being interrupted. "What do we have here?" he asked.

"We think this boy was trying to run away," said the soldier. "I have never seen him before, have you?"

"No," answered the corporal. "He must have run away from that troop that passed through here two days ago on their way to Baja California."

"Oh, no," said Miguel. "I came here with Father Serra and some boys jumped me and stole my clothes. They left me with these."

"A likely story," said the corporal. "Who is Father Serra? Let's go through your pockets and see what you have."

When the corporal searched Miguel's pockets he pulled out a knife. "Aha, look at this," he cried. "This is my knife that has been missing for two days."

"I didn't take it," protested Miguel. "Those boys must have stolen it. One was named Rafael."

"I don't know any Rafael," said the corporal.

"Come on, you are are going to spend some time in the stockade until we decide what to do with you."

"Should we ask Captain Portolá or Captain Rivera about him?" asked the soldier.

"No, we shouldn't bother either of them," answered the corporal. "I need a boy to polish my boots and take care of my horse. This one will do, so he can just stay here with us. Take him to the stockade for now."

"But, Corporal, he's hurt. He shouldn't be in the stockade until his wounds have healed." Miguel looked around and saw a boy about his age.

"Okay, Juan," said the corporal. "You take care of him but be sure he doesn't run off."

The corporal and other soldiers left and Miguel was alone with Juan. Juan got a bowl of water and using a cloth, carefully washed away the blood from Miguel's face. He tore the cloth in half and laid the wet cloths on Miguel's eye and on the lump on his head.

Juan was short and had straight black hair like Rafael, but his dark eyes were warm and friendly, not steely and hostile as Rafael's had been.

"Thank you," said Miguel, "but I need to get back to Father Serra. He will be worried about me and he might need my help."

"You need to lie still right now," said Juan. "And don't be thinking of leaving. Then we both would be in trouble. I know Rafael. He runs the streets looking for things to steal whenever he can get away from his duties with the soldiers. It must have been his friends you ran into. I heard that he was in trouble because of stealing. He probably traded clothes with you so he could escape punishment. It was pretty clever of him to put the knife he stole into your pocket. Anyway, right now you had better stay with us until we can prove your innocence."

"Why do you believe me and the soldiers wouldn't?" asked Miguel.

"I know Rafael's reputation and besides you talk a little differently than we do. The soldiers don't pay much attention to us boys. They are too ready to look at the circumstantial evidence. They don't care much about us anyway as long as we don't steal too much from them and do the work they want us to do," answered Juan.

"I'm going to find Rafael and get back at him for this," said Miguel.

"Would your Father Serra want you to get revenge?" asked Juan quietly.

"No, he wouldn't. He'd want me to forgive Rafael, but I find that hard to do right now," answered Miguel.

"Well, it's time to go to evening prayers and mass," said Juan.

"Do you go to church?" asked Miguel.

"Of course," answered Juan. "I'm a Christian Indian. My father was a Spanish soldier and my mother an Aztec Indian. I was baptized and have been confirmed in the church. I'd like to be a priest, but I'm not sure they will let me because I'm half Indian."

The two boys went to church, and after mass Juan took Miguel to the dining hall. The beans, hot chiles and tortillas tasted good to Miguel. He hadn't realized how hungry he was.

"Tomorrow I'll show you how to do the chores for the corporal, and perhaps he will forget about the knife and the stockade," said

Juan.

Miguel liked the Indian boy and was grateful for his kindness and consideration. He thought of Rafael who was also an Indian and how different he was from Juan. Miguel wondered how to get back to Father Serra, but he was so confused by the big city that he didn't know which way to go. Also he didn't want to make trouble for Juan. He noticed that the soldiers kept an eye on him. When he and Juan went to bed in the barracks he heard the click of a lock in the door. So he resigned himself to his fate for the time being.

Chapter 8

Life with the Soldiers

For many days after that Juan taught Miguel how to polish the soldiers' boots and buttons and shine their swords. Miguel helped Juan take care of the horses. He fed them and brushed their coats until they shone. They cleaned and oiled the saddles and bridles. The stables had to be cleaned every day. Miguel learned to wash the soldiers' clothes and clean the barracks. Sometimes they helped the cooks in the kitchen.

In return the boys had plenty to eat and could ride the horses. They trained along with the soldiers and were issued uniforms of sorts. The soldiers wore leather jackets which the

Indians' arrows could not pierce. For this reason they earned the nickname "Leather jackets". Juan and Miguel learned to shoot and clean the muskets. In some ways Miguel enjoyed his life with the soldiers, but he still thought about Father Serra. He considered running away, but he had no idea of how to get back to him.

Months passed and one day Juan said, "I've heard of your Father Serra. He is famous for giving excellent sermons in the cathedral and everyone goes to hear him."

"Oh, I must go and tell him where I am and what I have been doing," said Miguel.

"No, that's impossible," answered Juan. "He has gone to the Sierra Gordo to work with the Pame Indians. The Sierra Gordo is a wild section of Mexico."

Miguel was disappointed and sad that Father Serra had not been sent to California as he wished. He missed him and his kind ways. He wondered if he would ever see him again and if either one of them would ever get to California.

Several years passed while Miguel worked

for the soldiers. He learned to be a good soldier's helper and was well-liked and respected as an honest hard worker. He and Juan were close friends.

"Guess what?" shouted Juan excitedly one day. "I've just come from cleaning the rooms of Captain Rivera. Captain Portolá was there and I heard them talking. They had been to visit

the viceroy. The viceroy has orders from the King of Spain. As you know the viceroy takes the place of King Carlos in Mexico. The orders were about an expedition to California. Captain Portolá is to be the commander. Captain Rivera is going, too. And..... you will never guess, Miguel, who else is going."

"No," said Miguel. "I probably will never guess."

Juan paused to keep him in suspense. "Father Serra is going!" he exclaimed. "He will be in charge of converting and civilizing the Indians. He is to establish missions at San Diego and at Monterey. There will be two ships to carry supplies and two expeditions by land. Captain Rivera is going first, then Captain Portolá and Father Serra. I'm sure we can go, too. They'll need all the help they can get."

Miguel was speechless with delight. To think of seeing Father Serra again! He wanted to be able to work with him and help him. At last their dream of going to California might come true. He hoped he'd be able to let his father know. He knew Father Serra would be very happy.

"When do we leave?" he asked Juan.

"In a few days. First we'll travel to Loreto in Lower California. I heard them say that from there we'll go to San Diego in Upper California and then on to Monterey. The king wants Father Serra to establish missions there to convert the Indians and to colonize California."

"Why did he decide this all of a sudden?" wondered Miguel. "Father Serra and I have dreamed of going to California for so long, and now it seems that it's finally coming true."

"I heard Captain Portolá say that the King of Spain is worried that the English and the Russians will settle in California and claim it for their own. Even though it has been two hundred years since that English pirate, Francis Drake, landed somewhere in California, King Carlos thinks that the English may try to establish colonies on the California coast as they did on the Atlantic coast. There are thirteen colonies on the other side of the country that belong to England. Also the Russians have been coming down the California coast to hunt for otter. They may try to establish a colony. If they can settle in California, they might try to come to Mexico and steal the gold here."

The soldiers were very busy getting ready for the trip to Lower California. Some of them grumbled about leaving Mexico City and their Indian wives. They worried about going to a strange, uncharted land with hostile Indians.

"There is nothing in California," they said. "The Indians have no cities like they did in Mexico and there's no gold."

Others were happy about the preparations. "It'll be an adventure," they said. "No one's settled there before. Who knows what we might find. Perhaps we will be able to get land for ourselves."

Chapter 9

Back with Father Serra

The soldiers kept the boys busy getting ready for the expedition. Clean this, shine that, be sure the horses and mules are in good shape, was all they heard from morning to night. Finally everything was ready. Juan and Miguel were assigned mules to ride. Miguel was glad that he got his favorite mule, Diablo. They helped pack the mules and burros with supplies. They also took herds of cattle, sheep and goats to keep at the missions that were to be established.

As they assembled early in the morning of their departure, Miguel saw a short lame priest limping up to Portolá. Miguel shouted out,

"Father Serra, Father Serra, it's me, Miguel, Ramón's son!"

Father Serra turned and stared. A happy smile spread across his face and his eyes shone with pleasure. "Miguel," he said, "Miguel, my son. How glad I am to see you. Where have you been? What have you been doing? Are you a soldier now? I have been busy with the Pame Indians, but now I am going to California."

"Father, I was kept with the soldiers against my will. I never meant to leave you. It is a long story. Please believe me," begged Miguel.

"Of course, I believe you. Thanks be to God that you are alive and well. I will write your father in Majorca at once. I feared the worse for you," said Father Serra.

"I am so glad to see you. How is your leg? You are still limping. Are you going to walk to California or will you go on one of the ships?" asked Miguel.

"Of course I will walk to California and I will ask Captain Portolá to let you come with me."

"Oh, Father, please ask if my friend, Juan, can come with us. He is a good Christian

71

Indian and will be of much help. He helped me learn to be a soldier."

The corporal grumbled about losing two good helpers, but he could not refuse Father Serra and Captain Portolá. Father Serra and Miguel told each other about their adventures while they were separated.

"I prayed for you every day, my son," said Father Serra.

"I thought about you, too, Father, and wished I could get word to you that I was all right. They thought I had stolen the corporal's knife, and that I had been a helper to some other soldiers and had run away. So they made me work for them for punishment."

"I know you would not steal, Miguel," said Father Serra. "You are with me now and everything will be all right. I learned a great deal working with the Pame Indians and it will help me when I work with the Indians of California."

The expedition left for Baja (Lower) California and arrived in the city of Loreto. The two ships, the San Antonio and the San Carlos set sail for San Diego Bay. Everyone tried to persuade Father Serra to go on one of the ships because of his sore leg.   Naturally he refused. "I will walk to Alta (Upper) California," he said.

Captain Rivera prepared to leave with the expedition to San Diego by land.   Miguel and Juan worked hard to help load the mules.   A group of Indian workers came with Captain Rivera and were to accompany them to California.   They would help the expedition and to act as go-betweens with the California Indians.   As Miguel saddled a mule he caught sight of a tall Indian who looked familiar.   The Indian acted in a suspicious way, and Miguel noticed that he slyly slipped something from a jacket that one of the soldiers had taken off and hung on a bush.   Miguel was about to go up to the soldier to warn him when the Indian saw Miguel and quickly ducked around a building.

Miguel shouted, "Stop, thief," and ran after him.   But when he turned the corner, the Indian was nowhere to be seen.   Miguel went back and told the soldier what had happened. They both went to report it to Captain Rivera.

"All these Indians steal every chance they get," said Captain Rivera bitterly.   "We leave in the morning. If you spot him, grab him and bring him to me."

Miguel told Juan about the incident. "I'm sure that it was Rafael," Miguel said. "He's up to his old tricks. He's the one who stole the corporal's knife and left me to take the blame back in Mexico City."

"We must tell Father Serra," said Juan.

When Father Serra heard about it, he told the boys not to worry. They would catch up with Rafael in California.

"Yes, and when I do, I'm going to beat him within an inch of his life," said Miguel. "I'll get back at him for blaming me for his thievery."

A shadow came across Father Serra's face as he said quietly, "Miguel, remember that Rafael is an uncivilized Indian and he doesn't know any better. You must overlook his faults."

"He was supposed to be a Christian Indian, Father," said Miguel, "and he was with the soldiers, so he knows something of civilization and right from wrong. He wronged me, and I'll get even with him some day."

Father Serra said firmly, "Remember what

Jesus said. Forgive those who harm you."

Miguel said nothing because he didn't want to hurt Father Serra's feelings, but he felt in his heart that he couldn't forgive Rafael and he wanted his revenge.

Captain Portolá and Father Serra planned to lead the second expedition to San Diego by land. Father Crespi went with the first land expedition headed by Captain Rivera. Father Palou stayed behind again. Now he was the head of the mission in Loreto in Lower California.

"Write often, Junipero," said Father Palou, "and I will write to you. I will send you supplies if possible and perhaps I will join you in Upper California some day."

When the expedition was ready to leave Father Serra's leg was worse than ever. He could barely walk.

"You must ride a mule, Father Serra," ordered Captain Portolá, "or stay behind. You should stay here and let Father Palou take your place."

"No," said Father Serra, "I am going to go to California."

Juan and Miguel were very worried about him. They heard a mule braying in pain. Father Serra looked at the animal lying on the ground and saw that it, too, had a sore leg. The muleskinner in charge of the animals came up with a strong-smelling salve which he put on the mule's leg. In a short while the mule got up and walked about. It started eating as though nothing was wrong.

"Please use the same medication on my leg that you used on your mule," Father Serra said to the muleskinner.

"Oh, no, Father, I'm not a doctor and I don't know if this is good for people. I only know that it's good for animals," replied the muleskinner.

"Please," begged Father Serra. "No doctor has been able to help me. I am in great pain and I am desperate. I will not be able to go to California if my leg does not get better. Please help me."

So the muleskinner applied the medication called a poultice. He made the poultice of herbs and animal fat. It had to be applied hot, and Father Serra winced with pain as it was put on his sore leg.

Chapter 10

On to California

The next morning Father Serra's leg showed much improvement. The expedition set out for Upper California. The muleskinner and Captain Portolá insisted that Father Serra ride a mule and he finally agreed. Juan and Miguel helped him mount.

Before they left, another Indian boy named José Maria arrived to join them. He also was a Christian Indian like Juan. The three boys soon became good friends. José came from a different tribe than Juan and knew other Indian languages. He assisted the fathers with church duties and was very religious. He helped Father Serra serve mass.

As they traveled north they saw fewer settlements. The land was a desert and water and food were scarce. At first they saw no Indians. Then one day some Indians came into camp. They wore no clothes at all. Later they saw some Indian women who were completely covered.

José and Juan tried to ride up to one Indian boy to talk to him, but the boy was terrified of their mules and ran away. However, as the Indian boy watched the men and mules, he became less afraid and let José and Juan approach him. The boys tried to talk to him, but neither could understand one another.

The next day the Indian boy came again and even touched their mules. Juan and José decided to call him Flaco because he was so skinny. (Flaco means thin in Spanish.) Flaco was standing near a mule when he saw a rabbit in the bushes. Flaco suddenly jumped and grabbed his bow and arrows planning to shoot the rabbit. The mule was frightened at his sudden movement and shied away. The Indian thought this was very funny and unfortunately, began to tease the mules by running and yelling to scare them.

"Stop that, Flaco," ordered Juan, but the Indian boy did not listen.

This activity became very irritating to everyone because the Indians decided to keep up the sport of frightening the mules. Yelling and shouting they charged down upon them as the expedition was on its way. The animals scattered in all directions with their packs. Sometimes the packs loosened and fell off. The soldiers would have to round the animals up and load them again.

"Come, Diablo, come," called Miguel. When he, Juan, and José caught their mules, they would help catch the others.

Finally, the next time the Indians tried this, the soldiers fired their muskets into the air and scared the Indians off. Flaco and his friends came into camp that night. Miguel took off his boots and as he was rubbing his sore feet, Flaco grabbed his boots and ran off.

"Stop, thief," yelled Miguel and ran after him. José and some soldiers came to help. They finally retrieved the boots, but the Indians begged for their clothing and tried to take everything they could lay their hands on. Father Serra was trying to talk to a group of Indians to make friends with them. They were very curious about his glasses or spectacles as they were called in those days. He took them off to show them to the Indians. Suddenly the Indians and the glasses disappeared.

"What are you going to do now, Father?" asked Miguel. "you need your glasses. These Indians are awful thieves. They must be punished."

"No, no, Miguel," said Father Serra. "They are like children and need to be taught right from wrong. Let us not condemn them because they do not know any better. Come with me and we will look for my spectacles."

Juan, José, and Miguel went with Father Serra into the wilderness to find the Indians and the glasses. They arrived at an Indian village and by using sign language, they made the Indians understand what they were looking for. They went to several other villages. At the last village Miguel heard some Indian women quarreling loudly behind a hut. He went to investigate and found two women fighting over the glasses. One woman indicated that she wanted them for a headdress and the other wanted them for a necklace. Miguel tried to take the glasses away from them when they both began to hit him.

"Ouch!" he cried as he tried to hold them off without hitting back or hurting them and also trying to grab the glasses. The others heard the commotion and came running up.

"Wait!" said Father Serra as he took out two bead necklaces to exchange for the glasses. The women gave up the glasses for the necklaces and Father Serra and the boys returned to camp.

"You really looked funny fighting with those Indian ladies, Miguel," said Juan.

"Yes," said José. "We'll tell the soldiers what a fierce fighter you are."

Miguel jumped on José and knocked him down. Holding him down, Miguel shouted, "No, don't you dare tell anyone."

"I think those Indian ladies liked you, Miguel," teased Juan. "They left you something to remember them by."

Miguel stood up, releasing José. "What do

you mean, Juan?" he asked.

"I am talking about the scratches on your face and arms," laughed Juan.

"Now, boys," said Father Serra, "don't be mean. We have my spectacles back and we are all right. So let's forget about this incident."

The four adventurers returned to camp with no more talk. However, José and Juan would not let Miguel forget his encounter with the Indian women and teased him at every opportunity, whenever Father Serra was too busy to notice.

Chapter 11

San Diego

After many days of traveling they arrived at the port of San Diego. It was the year 1769, seven years before the United States of America declared its independence from England. The happenings on the other side of the continent were of little interest to those in California. Also people in the United States knew little about what was going on in California.

Miguel saw two ships in the harbor, but everything was strangely silent and there was no activity. The soldiers fired their guns and finally heard some answering shots. As they rode into camp, Captain Rivera and his men came out to greet them. Captain Rivera said that many had the disease, scurvy, on the ships. All of the crew of the San Carlos died except the cook. Many of the crew of the San Antonio were sick. Also, they had been unable to find the port of Monterey.

"We must find Monterey," said Father Serra. "Vizcaino found it a hundred years ago, so we should be able to find it again. The king wishes a mission to be established here in San Diego and one at Monterey. We must obey his orders. We must claim Upper California again for Spain so that Russia and England cannot claim it for their countries. But first we will take care of the sick and begin to build shelters and a church. We need to make friends with the local Indians and begin to teach them."

Miguel kept his eyes open for Rafael but did not see him. However, he did see the soldier from whom Rafael had stolen the knife. "Have you seen that thief?" asked Miguel.

"No," said the soldier. "He was with us part of the way from Loreto, but he kept away from me, and we were all too busy setting up camp every night and too tired from traveling all day to apprehend him. Then one day when we were close to San Diego, I heard that he and several other Indians from Mexico ran away from us and joined the local wild Indian tribes here in California."

"Too bad," said Miguel, "but I'll catch up with him yet."

"Well, he took an old dull knife," said the soldier, "and I have another better one, so I'm not worried about him."

I am, thought Miguel, I still want to get back at Rafael.

The boys helped Father Serra set up a large wooden cross and built an altar with a roof of branches over it. They hung a bell from a branch of a tree and Father Serra rang it and called the Indians to come. José, Juan, and Miguel worked hard to help build huts and to lay out the foundation for the church. They planted seeds and grapevine and fruit tree seedlings.

They still had time for fun, though, especially to play tricks on each other. One morning Miguel woke up to find his clothes tied into knots. Another time Juan bit into a tortilla and found it full of leaves. Then José went to wash himself and the bucket was full of mud instead of water. The boys also enjoyed watching the Indians dance and act out battles or

hunting events.

Father Serra tried hard to learn the Indian languages. The Indians came into camp every day to beg and to steal. They were very curious and always wanted food. They usually took the food off into the woods to eat. They also wanted the soldiers' clothes.

José, Juan and Miguel tried to talk to the Indians, too. Juan and José could learn the languages more easily because some were similar to their own Indian dialects. Miguel found it as hard as Father Serra did to learn to speak with the Indians. Sometimes sign language was enough. They taught the Indians to speak Spanish so everyone was learning each others' languages. Father Serra was unhappy that he couldn't convert the Indians faster and that there had been no baptisms. He worried about the Indians dying without being baptized. The boys tried to persuade the Indians to bring their babies in to be baptized.

One day José brought some Indians into camp with a baby boy to be baptized. Two soldiers agreed to be godparents. Some of the Indians stayed partly hidden in the bushes.

Miguel observed each one carefully and thought he saw Rafael hiding behind a tree. The Indians stood around to watch the ceremony, but just as Father Serra was ready to pour the holy water over the baby, an Indian grabbed the little one and ran away. Miguel thought it was Rafael.

Father Serra was very disappointed and discouraged, but he did not give up. "I am going to the Indians in their villages," he said. "I will take Miguel, Juan, and José with me."

"You're crazy," said one of the soldiers. "The Indians will kill you."

The four set out and soon a group of Indian warriors surrounded them. The warriors were ready to kill them. Miguel's knees shook and he tried to see if he could recognize Rafael among them, but several had painted their faces.

"Everyone just stand still and stay calm," ordered Father Serra in a low voice. "José, see if you can communicate with them."

José used sign language and the few words he had learned to convince the Indians that the soldiers would come to avenge them if they were killed. Miguel breathed a sigh of relief when the Indians left.

A few days later another large group of Indians advanced upon them with warlike intentions. This time Miguel wasn't quite so frightened.

Again Father Serra said, "Stay calm and don't make any threatening moves. Take out the banner with the picture of Mary and Jesus. Slowly unfurl it so the Indians can see it."

The Indians were astonished as they had never seen a picture like that before. They thought this was the white man's magic and were afraid, so they did not harm the little group. Miguel noticed one

Indian who did not pay much attention to the banner, and he tried to get near enough to see if it was Rafael. But the tall Indian melted into the forest and Miguel did not dare to follow him alone.

After visiting many villages the four adventurers returned to San Diego. The church was built and Father Serra began teaching the Indian children. Many weeks later José was resting under some manzanita bushes when he overheard a group of Indians talking. By this time he was fairly proficient in their language and could understand almost everything they were saying.

"Let us test the power of this small white man with his cross and talk of his God," said one in a low voice.

"Yes, I would like to see how his power would stand up to our poison," agreed another.

"We can put it in the berry juice that is called wine that he drinks when he is in the church saying mass," said the first voice. José leaped to his feet in shock forgetting to move quietly.

"What is that?" cried one Indian. "Who is

there?"

The group ran out of the hut and saw José starting to run away. Unfortunately he tripped over a root and fell. The Indians caught up with him and soon overpowered him. They tied his hands behind his back and hastily put a gag over his mouth. Before they did, he managed to shout, "Juan, Miguel, they are going to hurt Father Serra." The Indians dragged him into the hut as Juan and Miguel came running up to see what the commotion was. The group soon had them tied and gagged also.

The Indians left them in the hut and went to carry out their plan. The three struggled to get loose. Finally Miguel managed to free José. As soon as he removed the gag José told the others of the plot. They set Juan free and the boys all ran to the church.

They had barely entered when they saw Father Serra collapse in front of the altar. Father Crespi and others ran to help him. They carried him to his room and laid him on his cot. The boys quickly told Father Crespi what they knew. The doctor offered Father Serra an antidote but he refused it. He couldn't talk and lay very still. Everyone was afraid that he would die. The boys worried all night, but the next morning Father Serra had recovered.

"Why wouldn't you take the antidote, Father?" asked Miguel.

"I never take any medicine like that," answered Father Serra. "I trust in God to take care of me." The boys and the soldiers searched for the guilty Indians, but they were never found. Of course Father Serra forgave them anyway.

One day a strange silence hung over the settlement. All the Indians disappeared. The quiet persisted for several days Then at dawn warwhoops broke the silence as the Indians attacked. Arrows flew all around and the soldiers answered with gunshots. Father Serra called to the boys to come into the church for safety. Showers of arrows fell around them, and José cried out, "I'm hit!" Miguel and Juan carried him into the church where he died in Father Serra's arms. Father Crespi put his hand out by the door and an arrow pierced it. The wound bothered him the rest of his life.

Everyone prayed and the few soldiers kept shooting at the attacking Indians. Then, just as suddenly as they had come, the Indians left. They took their dead and wounded with them.

Miguel, Juan, and Father Serra grieved for José and gave him a Christian burial behind the church. Miguel wanted to get a gun and go after the murderers, but Father Serra said, "No, these Indians are afraid of us. That is why they try to hurt us. We must make friends with them and show them that we mean them no harm. José would want us to forgive them and try to help them."

The next day the Indians returned carrying their wounded into the settlement. The priests tended their wounds and tried to heal them. At first Miguel would not go near the wounded Indians. He was still too angry that his friend, José, had been killed. However, when he heard an Indian groaning with pain in one hut and Father Serra's voice trying to comfort him, he went in to see what was happening.

"I'm afraid that this one will not recover," said Father Serra. It was all Miguel could do to keep from saying that he hoped the Indian would die. Then the Indian said something in Spanish.

"You speak our language!" said Father Serra in surprise.

"Yes, Father, please make me well. I do not want to die."

Miguel came closer to look at the Indian lying on a cot. "Rafael," he cried, "so, you thief! I have finally found you."

"Don't let him hurt me," begged Rafael fearfully. "I'm sorry for what I did, Miguel. Father, help me. Please forgive me."

"Forgive him, Miguel," said Father Serra. "He is begging you. He does not have long to live."

Miguel hesitated, then looking at Father Serra's anxious face and into his kind eyes, said, "All right, Rafael, I forgive you, and I'm sorry that you're hurt so badly."

"Thank you," answered Rafael, "now, Father, will you forgive me too? The raid was my idea and I persuaded the Indians to attack. We wanted your weapons, food, and clothing. I also told them to stop you from baptizing the baby. I think that from now on they will not be so hostile to you."

"You are forgiven," said Father Serra. "You have confessed your sins and our Father in heaven will forgive you, too."

Rafael breathed his last and also was buried behind the church. Without their leader and with the fathers helping the wounded, the Indians gave them no more trouble for the time being. They no longer begged and stole, but came to learn Spanish and be converted to the Christian religion.

Chapter 12

The Search for Monterey

"I wonder where Captain Portolá is," said Juan as he and Miguel were carrying firewood to the settlement.

"Yes, I wonder that and also why our supply ship, the San Antonio, is not here yet," answered Miguel. "If we don't get some supplies soon, we'll not have enough food and we'll have to abandon San Diego and return to Mexico."

"That would break Father Serra's heart," said Juan. "He was sad enough when José was killed, but now he has been much happier with so many Indians coming in to be converted."

97

Suddenly the boys heard a commotion over the hill. "It must be Captain Portolá and his men," shouted Miguel.

"There they are, and Father Crespi, too," added Juan. "Let's go and meet them."

The men in the settlement heard their shouts and everyone came out to greet the travelers. "Did you find Monterey? How is everything? Was it a hard trip? Did you find many Indians? Where are the mules? Whew, you all smell like mules."

The returning group of men lay on the ground exhausted. Captain Portolá held up his hand for silence. "First we need food," he said. "We smell like mules and the mules are not here because we ate them. We never found Monterey Bay. I don't think there is such a place. The maps must be wrong."

"We did find a much larger bay farther north," said Father Crespi. "I named it San Francisco."

"Where is the supply ship, the San Antonio?" demanded Captain Portolá.

"We're still waiting for it," answered Father Serra.

"It will probably never come," said Captain Portolá. "Our supplies are almost gone. We must prepare to return to Mexico or we will starve."

Father Serra begged Portolá to wait a little longer. "Let us pray for nine more days until it is the feast of St. Joseph (San José)."

Captain Portolá did not want to stay even one more day. "We should leave at once," he said.

"I will not leave," said Father Serra.

"You can't stay here by yourself," said Captain Portolá.

"I'll stay, too," said Father Crespi, "Father Serra will not be by himself."

Juan and Miguel overheard the conversation. "I'll be glad to get back to Mexico," said Juan.

"How can you say that?" asked Miguel. "Don't you see how sad Father Serra is at the thought of leaving? In fact, he plans to stay even if the soldiers go. I'm going to stay with him."

"Don't be crazy," said Juan. "You'll die of starvation if the Indians don't kill you first."

"I can't leave Father Serra," insisted Miguel stubbornly. "My father was his good friend back home on the island of Majorca. He wanted to come here to California with Father Serra, but he had to stay home and take care of our family, so I came instead. I can't leave Father Serra. I would not only be letting Father Serra down, but also my own father."

"Well, I'll stay, too, and we had better pray a great deal," said Juan.

Every day Juan, Miguel, Father Serra, and Father Crespi climbed the hill overlooking San Diego Bay to look for the ship. On the ninth day they celebrated the feast of St., Joseph.

"Tomorrow we must return to Mexico," announced Captain Portolá.

Father Serra went one more time to scan the ocean for the missing ship. Suddenly he spotted a sail on the horizon. There was the San Antonio! "The ship!" he shouted. Juan and Miguel ran up the hill to see.

"It is the San Antonio," They shouted together, jumping up and down in excitement. First they waved to the sailors on the ship and then waved and shouted to the soldiers in the

settlement. The ship dropped anchor and Captain Perez and his crew brought supplies to the beach in the small boats. "I was trying to find Monterey," explained Captain Perez, "but when I failed, I came here to see what was happening. I have brought more seeds, plants, fruit trees, and grape vines. Soon you'll grow your own food and have no need of ships to bring you provisions."

After the supplies were unloaded, Captain Perez said that he had orders to find Monterey and that Father Serra was to go with him. "May I go, too, Father?" asked Miguel.

"Of course, Miguel," answered Father Serra, "I don't know what I would do without you."

Later Miguel and Juan were talking about the expedition. "What about you, Juan, don't you want to go too?" asked Miguel.

"I think I will stay here in San Diego," answered Juan. "I am used to it here and it is closer to Lower California and Mexico. There is plenty of work here."

"I know why you want to stay," teased Miguel. "I saw Maria smiling at you, and you had a very silly look on your face." Juan's face grew red and he jumped on Miguel. The two boys rolled over and over on the ground.

"Okay, Juan, you win," gasped Miguel. "Let me up."

"I do like Maria," Juan admitted. "Perhaps we will marry some day. I am old enough, you know."

"Maria is a beautiful girl," said Miguel. "It is too bad that her parents and many of her tribe died from sickness. You wouldn't think the Indians would die so easily from simple illnesses like measles, but I guess they're not used to the diseases we have always had."

"Father Serra is happy that at least they become Christians and are baptized before they die so that they will go to heaven. I'm glad that I am going with him to Monterey. He'll be overjoyed to be able to convert more Indians."

"I'll be sorry to see you go," said Juan. "But maybe you'll come back some day."

"Oh, probably," said Miguel, "Father Serra wants to establish a mission in Monterey and then a whole string of missions between San Diego and Monterey. He is so determined that I am sure he will."

Father Serra and Miguel sailed for Monterey. When they arrived where they thought it should be according to the map, Captain Portolá realized that he had passed by it before without knowing it. Father Serra decided that the mission should be built on the Carmel River and he named it San Carlos Mission. He decided to build another mission by the large bay called San Francisco. That would honor St. Francis(San Francisco) who was the founding father of the Franciscan order of priests to which Father Serra belonged.

San Carlos is a beautiful place. Father Serra especially loved the wild roses that grew there and he found wild grapes, too. San Carlos was always his favorite mission and became his headquarters in California.

One day some Indians came to the mission carrying a badly wounded member of their tribe. "What happened?" asked Father Serra.

One of the Indians who spoke a little Spanish answered, "A large grizzly bear attacked him. He was hunting rabbits, but accidentally got too close to a female with cubs and she almost killed him."

"Come, let me tend to his wounds," said Father Serra.

"Let's kill the bears for food," Miguel suggested. "Then it will be safer for everyone and we can use the meat and skins." Miguel was growing up and could shoot as well as any soldier. Father Serra agreed with this idea so Miguel and several soldiers went to the valley where there were many bears. They named the place Los Osos which means the bears in Spanish.

"We must be careful," said the corporal. "Even though we have guns these bears are dangerous."

The horses were very nervous and hard to manage when they caught the scent of the bears. Suddenly a horse reared and threw off his rider. The soldier fell very close to a large male grizzly. The bear roared, growled and charged the fallen soldier. The corporal shot at the grizzly, but it just paused, shook himself, and charged on toward the dazed man. Then Miguel fired and luckily hit a vital spot. The vicious bear dropped dead just a few feet from the stunned soldier. The grateful soldier roused himself and shouted his thanks to Miguel. Miguel helped him to recover his frightened horse and remount.

The Spanish soldiers killed many grizzly bears. The Indians were happy because the grizzlies killed and wounded many Indians every year. In gratitude the Indians began coming to the mission in great numbers.

Father Serra converted many to Christianity and baptized them. This made him very happy.

One evening as Miguel helped bring the cattle in to the pens for the night, he saw some people coming from the harbor. The ship must be in from San Diego, he thought. He hurried to meet them hoping to hear news of Juan and Maria.

"Ho, Miguel, don't you recognize me?" called out Juan.

"Juan, I'm so glad to see you," answered Miguel. The two friends embraced and Miguel kissed Maria's cheek. Then he noticed the bundle she was carrying. "What is this?" he asked.

"Our son, Ramón," answered Maria shyly.

"I named him for your father, Miguel, because you talked about him so much that I felt I knew him," said Juan.

"That makes me very happy," answered Miguel. "Come, we must go to Father Serra and bring him the news."

"Unfortunately I have bad news," said Juan. Miguel noticed tears in Maria's eyes.

"What is it?" Miguel asked.

"Wait until we tell everyone at once so we don't have to repeat the sad story and we can answer questions," said Juan.

Everyone gathered in the large dining room in the fathers' quarters. "Indians attacked San Diego Mission," announced Juan. "They killed one of the fathers and destroyed the church. They stole many religious articles and ruined other parts of the mission."

The news shocked everyone. Father Serra was very upset. "San Diego must be rebuilt at once," he said. "I will talk to Governor Fages."

The next day when Miguel walked past Father Serra's room, he heard voices. "We need to establish more missions soon," said Father Serra. "We need one at San Buenaventura and another at Santa Barbara especially as those missions would be half way between San Carlos and San Diego. Also we must rebuild San Diego as soon as possible."

"We don't have enough soldiers to guard them," answered Governor Fages. "We need to build forts first. Perhaps we should abandon San Diego entirely."

"Never!" said Father Serra. "God will provide protection and the Indians will be friendly if they are well-treated. It is when the soldiers mistreat them that they retaliate by attacking us. Many Indians welcome our presence here in California."

"I am against rebuilding San Diego and it is

impossible to begin building more missions right now," announced Governor Fages.

"We must build more missions and rebuild San Diego," argued Father Serra stubbornly. "The viceroy in Mexico and the King of Spain both told me that we should do this as soon as possible. Otherwise we may lose Alta California to foreigners."

Governor Fages stomped away angrily and Father Serra went into the church to pray for his missions.

Chapter 13

Trouble at San Carlos

"I must go to Mexico," said Father Serra. "Do you want to go with me, Miguel?"

"If you don't mind, Father, I would rather stay here at San Carlos," said Miguel. "I like to hunt bears and other wild animals. Also I want to continue to teach the Indians how to raise crops and tend the livestock."

"A good choice, Miguel," said Father Serra, "I will miss you, but you are needed more here, and I was hoping you would decide to stay."

"I'll miss you, too, Father," answered Miguel. "Why do you have to go?"

"The missions are not being built fast enough. The commandantes here believe that there are not enough soldiers to guard against hostile Indians so they refuse to build more missions. I want to convince the viceroy in Mexico City to send more missionaries, more soldiers, and more supplies to California. There are so many Indians to be converted, and this is such a beautiful land that we do not want to lose what we have already gained. We must rebuild San Diego Mission as soon as possible."

"Do you think the viceroy will help you?" asked Miguel.

"Yes," answered Father Serra, "don't forget he takes the place of the king here in the New World and the army must obey his orders. He is anxious to build towns in California so it will be settled for Spain."

"I'm glad you're going by ship," said Miguel. "That way your leg can have a good rest and perhaps it will really heal at last."

Father Serra left for Mexico and Miguel stayed at Mission San Carlos. Juan and his family returned to San Diego to help with the rebuilding. There was always so much to be done. Miguel helped the soldiers and the priests teach the Indians how to make adobe bricks for the many buildings that were need-ed. They taught the Indians how to plow the soil and plant vegetables. The Indians learned to spin wool, weave cloth and make clothes and blankets. They taught them to prepare food in

the Spanish and Mexican ways.

Even Father Serra worked alongside the Indians to make adobe bricks and work in the fields. He taught himself how to sew so that he could teach the Indians to make clothes.

Miguel liked most of the Indians and it made him feel proud and important to be able to teach the Indian boys. Often his Indian friends showed him new places to hunt and fish and told him of their tribal customs. Sometimes he envied their old way of life when they didn't have to work or spend so much time in church. But Miguel did not always get along with the soldiers and he disliked their cruelty to the Indians. Father Serra defended the Indians from the soldiers' brutal ways. He believed that the soldiers should live separate from the Indians and the mission.

One day Miguel heard screams of pain and saw a soldier beating a young Indian boy with a stick.

"What are you doing?" asked Miguel.

"This lazy good-for-nothing Pablo won't work today," answered the soldier whose name was Esteban. "I am teaching him a lesson."

"Why won't you work?" Miguel asked the Indian.

"I'm sick. My arms and legs hurt and so does my head," answered Pablo.

"He can't work because he is sick. You shouldn't beat a sick person," said Miguel to the soldier.

"Ha, he is just faking," said Esteban and he began to hit the boy again.

"You would not do that if Father Serra were here," said Miguel. "You'd better stop."

"Who's going to make me?" sneered the soldier.

"I am," said Miguel as he grabbed the stick and swung at the soldier who doubled up his fists and struck back. The two exchanged blows.

"Fight, fight," shouted the workers. Everyone dropped their tools and ran to gather around to watch. Soon the corporal ran up and pulled the two fighters apart.

"What's going on here?" he demanded.

"This young fool jumped me," growled the soldier.

"He was beating this Indian boy," said

Miguel.

"Of course," said Esteban, "Pablo wouldn't work and I was punishing him. They have to learn who's the boss around here."

"Don't be so hard on the Indians," the corporal said to Esteban, "and you, Miguel, don't interfere in matters that do not concern you."

"Father Serra does not allow you to mistreat the Indians," said Miguel.

"Well, Father Serra is not here right now and we have to keep discipline as well as we can. Miguel, you can spend the night in the guardhouse to help you learn to mind your own business," ordered the corporal.

"These Indians need more punishment," said Esteban.

The soldiers laughed and sneered at Miguel as the corporal led him off. Miguel spent an unpleasant night locked up in the jail. The jail was a large room connected to the soldiers' quarters inside the mission walls. He could hear the jeers of the soldiers in the nearby barracks.

"The presidio (fort) should be located a few miles away from the mission and the Indian

houses," Father Serra had once said. "Then there would be less trouble from the soldiers."

A few days later Miguel noticed a soldier talking to a lovely young Indian girl. He was pulling her arm and she seemed unhappy and upset.

"No, leave me alone," he heard her say.

"Oh, come on, Carmelita," said the soldier, "just give me one little kiss."

Carmelita tried to pull away and the soldier slapped her and she began to cry.

"Stop that," said the soldier, "I won't hurt you if you be nice to me."

Miguel ran up, "Let her go," he ordered. The soldier turned around and Miguel saw that it was Esteban.

"You again," snarled Esteban, "haven't you learned to mind your own business yet? This time I'll teach you a lesson you won't forget." Esteban let go of the girl and swung at Miguel with his fist. Miguel ducked the blow and lashed back.

Carmelita ran to the mission courtyard where Father Crespi was standing in front of the church. "Oh, Father, come quick, Esteban was bothering me. Miguel told him to stop and now they are fighting," she cried.

"Calm down, child," said Father Crespi. "Tell me what happened."

"Esteban tried to make me kiss him and Miguel stopped him. They are fighting and Miguel will get hurt because Esteban is so much bigger than he is," said Carmelita. "They're out by the orchard."

"Go to the women's house and stay with the other women," ordered Father Crespi. "I will take care of this."

"Pablo," called Father Crespi, "go and bring the Corporal to the orchard."

Father Crespi ran to the orchard and found the two fighters bashing each other. "Stop," he ordered. The surprised men looked up and when they saw that it was Father Crespi, they stopped fighting.

"What is going on here?" asked Father Crespi.

"Miguel jumped me again," snarled Esteban.

"He was bothering Carmelita," explained Miguel.

"I was not," snapped Esteban.

"Be sure to tell the truth," said Father Crespi. "Carmelita has already complained to me about you, Esteban."

Just then the corporal came running up.

"Oh, so it's you again," he said when he saw Esteban and Miguel. "Didn't the night in the guardhouse do you any good?"

"Wait, corporal," said Father Crespi, "I don't think it's Miguel's fault. I have talked to Carmelita. Esteban was annoying her. Your soldiers must learn to leave the Indian women alone. They must not mistreat the Indians. The Indians are learning our ways and our religion. They are not the concern of soldiers. We priests are in charge of their welfare."

"Very well, Father," said the corporal. "This time Esteban can spend the night in the guardhouse."

The other soldiers who had gathered around, grumbled at this and glared at Miguel. Miguel heard Esteban mutter under his breath, "I'll get even with you."

Miguel's eye was beginning to swell and his nose was bloody. Esteban also had some bruises. The corporal escorted Esteban to the guardhouse. Miguel and Father Crespi walked to the church.

"You like these poor Indians, don't you?" asked Father Crespi.

"Yes, Father," answered Miguel. "They are so friendly and childlike. Father Serra always tries to help them. He hopes that they will all be brought into our religion."

"Go and wash the blood off and hold a wet cloth over your eye," said Father Crespi. "Also you had better look out for Esteban from now on. I'm afraid that you have made an enemy."

"You're right, Father, I will," said Miguel.

Miguel walked to the fountain in the middle of the mission garden. Carmelita and Pablo came up to him.

"Thank you for helping me," said Carmelita shyly. "My brother is grateful to you, too, for defending him against that bully, Esteban."

"I'm sorry you have been mistreated," said Miguel. "Not all soldiers are like Esteban."

"We know that," said Pablo, "but many soldiers are cruel and that's why some Indians run away and others think of attacking the missions. We like the fathers, but we hate the soldiers."

"The fathers teach us not to hate," answered Miguel. "But sometimes it's hard to do as they say."

Miguel thought Carmelita the prettiest girl he had ever seen. Her hair was long and shiny and as black as coal. Her eyes shone like stars and her face lit up like the sunlight when she smiled. He understood now why Juan stayed in San Diego and married Maria. Suddenly the church bell began to ring.

"Come," said Carmelita, "it's time for prayers. Let's go into the church together." Carmelita put her cool little hand on Miguel's arm, and he suddenly felt very warm all over. In church Miguel could not concentrate on the prayers. His head felt light and he thought he was going to faint. I must be coming down with some illness, he thought.

That night Miguel could hardly sleep and when he did doze off, he dreamed that Carmelita ran through the fields and he tried to catch her. Just as he was about to touch her arm he woke up with a start. What is the matter with me, he thought. I must be going crazy. The next morning Miguel tried to ease his mind by working hard.

"What are you doing?" asked Pablo. "Don't put water on the dry bricks. We want them to get hard. Put the water over here where we are mixing the mud to form the adobe bricks."

Miguel felt foolish and didn't know what to say. Then Carmelita walked by with a group of girls on their way to pick berries. She smiled at him and he felt his heart leap into his throat.

"Ha, Miguel, do you ever have a silly look on your face," teased Pablo. "That's just my sister. Do you think it's the queen of Spain?"

Miguel's face turned as red as a beet and he looked down. Carmelita is more beautiful than any queen, he thought to himself. A few evenings later Miguel strolled near the Indian women's house, dreaming of Carmelita, when suddenly a large form came out from behind a tree.

"No priest or girl will protect you this time," growled a voice from the darkness.

It's Esteban, thought Miguel as he put up his fists to defend himself. A punch to the jaw toppled him over onto the ground. He tasted blood as Esteban delivered a vicious kick to his side. Miguel grunted at the pain and began to crawl away from his attacker. Another kick sent him sprawling. A loud groan escaped his lips as he tried to get to his feet. Miguel became aware of a rustling noise among the bushes and the sound of running feet. As he got up Miguel saw several slim forms holding sticks and beating at Esteban.

"Ouch, stop!" yelled Esteban. He put up his hands to fend off the blows that were raining on him from all sides. "Let me be." He put his head down and butted through the encircled figures and ran off.

"Are you all right, Miguel?" asked one of his rescuers.

"Yes, you came just in time. Who's there?" asked Miguel.

"It's me, Pablo, I came with my friends to help you. I saw you walking in this direction and then I saw Esteban come after you. I knew he was up to no good, and you were in such a daze you didn't know he was there," said Pablo.

"Well, now we're even," said Miguel. "I helped you and now you have helped me."

"You're still ahead because of what you did for my sister," answered Pablo.

"That was nothing," said Miguel. "I would

do that a thousand times for Carmelita. I would die for her." All the Indians began to laugh and Miguel felt his face grow red.

"I would help any of you," said Miguel lamely as he tried to cover up his confusion.

The next morning Father Crespi noticed the new bruises on Miguel's face. "What happened, Miguel?" he asked.

"Oh, nothing much," answered Miguel.

"I think I'll examine Esteban today and see if there is 'nothing much' the matter with him, too," said Father Crespi.

When Father Crespi saw Esteban's black and blue marks he asked Pablo what happened. After Pablo told him the story, Father Crespi went to the corporal. "We must do something about Esteban," Father Crespi said. "He's a troublemaker. Either Miguel or some Indian might be either badly hurt or killed, and then there will be much trouble here."

"You are right," said the corporal. "I will send Esteban back to Mexico."

With Esteban gone peace returned to the mission.

Every morning the bells of the mission woke

everyone at sunrise. Miguel and Pablo went to church with the soldiers and Indians. After the morning mass the women served a breakfast of cornmeal mush. Then the Indians would go to work in the fields until noon. Miguel, the priests and sometimes some of the soldiers would go with them to teach them how to plant corn, beans, and other vegetables. The Indians learned to tend the grapevines, berry bushes and fruit trees.

Miguel helped Pablo and the other Indian boys learn to ride horses and herd the cattle and sheep. While the men worked in the fields, Carmelita and the Indian girls learned to cook and sew.

"You learn fast, Pablo," said Miguel. "With everyone working so hard we'll have plenty of food and the mission buildings will soon be completed. This is such a difference from when I first came to California. At San Diego we almost ran out of food before we could build the mission."

"I would really rather hunt and fish," answered Pablo. "But many of your ways are better than our old ways. Sometimes we didn't

have enough to eat and your adobe buildings are more comfortable in cold weather than our grass huts."

"When the harvest is over I'm going to learn more about your religion from Father Crespi," added Pablo. "My little brother and sister are learning to read and write and to sing songs in church. We have all been trying hard to learn to speak Spanish."

"I think you speak our language very well,"

said Miguel. "Well, let's go to lunch and I'll see you after siesta."

That evening Miguel saw Pablo and his brothers and sisters in the church for services after their dinner of meat and vegetables. He watched Carmelita walk to the special living quarters for the unmarried girls. The doors to their quarters were locked at night for their protection. Pablo lived in a hut outside the mission walls with the other unmarried Indian men. The married Indian couples with their small children also lived outside.

Miguel had a small room near the priests' quarters and usually ate his meals with the priests in the dining room by Father Serra's office.

Chapter 14

Father Serra Returns

A few weeks later Father Serra came back from Mexico with good news.

"I am glad to see you so happy, Father," said Miguel, "even though your leg is still sore and swollen."

"Never mind about that," said Father Serra. "The viceroy gave me permission to rebuild San Diego and to build more missions and he ordered that it be done quickly."

"That's wonderful," said Miguel, "and I have some news too."

"What is it, my son?" asked Father Serra.

"I wish to be married," answered Miguel. "Will you perform the ceremony?"

"Of course," said Father Serra. "Who do you want to marry?"

"I'm in love with Carmelita," said Miguel with a blush. "She has consented to marry me. I plan to apply to the Viceroy for a ranch. We will build a house close to the mission and stay here to work and help you."

"I'm glad to hear that," said Father Serra. "I need you more than ever with new missions to be built. I wish you could visit the other missions as I have. Each one is alike in some ways but different in others. As you know, they are usually built of adobe bricks and have the form of a quadrangle. We always build the church first at one corner of the quadrangle."

"I like the bell towers and the bells that come from Peru and Spain," said Miguel.

"Well, sometimes we have to put wooden bells in the towers just for looks until we can get real ones," remarked Father Serra. "Some of the missions are built of stone and we replaced the thatch roofs with tile so they don't burn so easily. I make sure that each mission is built near a river, too."

"It's nice that the cooking and baking is

129

done outdoors because of the fire danger and also it's cooler," said Miguel. "It was a good idea to put the rooms inside the walls for the different workshops."

"The Indians learned to make candles very well," said Father Serra. "They work hard in the spinning and weaving rooms, also in the saddle-making room. Everything we need is produced here."

"It is amazing how fast they learned and how hard they work," added Miguel. "You know, actually in many ways the mission looks like a fort with the high walls all around it."

"I hope it's a fort of peace and not war or evil," answered Father Serra.

Shortly after the wedding of Miguel and Carmelita Father Crespi fell ill. A few days later he died.

"Why did he have to die, Father? "asked Miguel. "He was even younger than you."

"I know, Miguel," answered Father Serra sadly, "but none of us knows when God will take us. I will miss him. Did I tell you that Father Crespi and Father Palou were students of mine in Majorca? Father Crespi and Father

Palou were childhood friends and my best friends, too.

Father Serra worked hard to continue building missions. Father Palou came to Upper California and now lived at the San Francisco Mission. However, they were both too busy to see each other very often.

One day Miguel noticed that Father Serra was preparing to leave again. "Where are you going, Father?" he asked.

"I am going to visit the other missions," answered Father Serra.

"Please go by ship," said Miguel, "or if you

refuse to do that, please take a horse or mule to ride on. Your leg is still not well."

"Don't worry about me," said Father Serra, "God will look after me."

Miguel sadly watched the little lame priest limp down El Camino Real(the King's Highway) on his way to visit his beloved missions. At each one he baptized and confirmed the Indians into the Christian religion. He listened to the reports of the priests and praised them for their hard work.

Father Serra stopped at Santa Barbara where the governor had already started to build the presidio (fort).

"We must start work on the mission now," said Father Serra.

"No," said the governor, "we must finish the presidio first."

"Since you are not going to build the mission, I am not needed here. I will return to San Carlos," said Father Serra.

Father Serra wrote a long letter to Father Palou telling him all about how to run the missions and what was needed to be done. He asked Father Palou to come to San Carlos to visit him. Father Palou came to San Carlos at once and saw that Father Serra was very weak. They prayed together and Father Palou tried to take over many of his tasks. One afternoon Father Palou went to his hut and found that Father Serra had peacefully died in his sleep.

The mission bells rang out and the guns of the ships in the harbor sounded out the news. Miguel and Carmelita wept at the loss of the beloved priest. All the Indians came to say goodbye as did the soldiers and sailors from the ships. Father Serra was buried under the altar in the church.

The next year Carmelita and Miguel had a son. They named him Miguel for his father and for Father Serra.

"Perhaps our son will become a priest like Father Serra," Miguel said to Carmelita.

"No one can be like Father Serra," answered Carmelita, "but we shall see."

Miguel and Carmelita had a large happy family. They lived on their ranch near San Carlos. Miguel told his children stories of his life with Father Serra so they grew up feeling as if they had known the little priest, too.

EPILOGUE

Father Serra established nine missions in his lifetime. The first at San Diego in 1769 and the second was at San Carlos at Carmel in 1770. Father Serra had his headquarters at San Carlos and spent most of his time there. It was his favorite mission. The other missions that he personally founded are San Francisco, Santa Clara, San Antonio, San Luis Obispo, San Buenaventura, San Gabriel, and San Juan Capistrano. Father Serra wanted to build a mission at Santa Barbara very badly, but it was not built until after his death.

Father Serra died in 1784. By 1823 twenty-one missions were built in California from San Diego to San Francisco. Each mission was about a day's journey apart. Thousands of Indians were baptized and became Christians.

After 1823 there was less support for the

missions and they fell into ruins. In 1826 the first Americans came to California. The Gold Rush of 1849 brought many people to California. In 1850 California became a state of the United States. No one paid much attention to the old ruined missions. Some were used as stables for horses or as hideouts for bandits.

But towns had sprung up around the missions and one day the government of the United States began to rebuild and restore them. So now you can visit all 21 missions and see how they were during the mission days.

The End

BIBLIOGRAPHY

Ainsworth, Katherine and Edward, In the Shade of the Juniper Tree: A Life of Fray Junipero Serra, Doubleday, 1960

Bolton, Ivy May, Father Junipero Serra, Julian Messner, Inc. 1952

Demarest, Donald, The First Californian: The Story of Fray Junipero Serra, 1963

Duque, Sally, Sally and Father Serra, Binfords & Mort, 1958

Englebert, Omer, The Last of the Conquistadors, Harcourt, 1956

Fitch, Abigail H., Junipero Serra, The Man and His Work, A. C. McClurg & Co., 1914

Geiger, Maynard, (TR) Palou's Life of Fray Junipero Serra, Academy of American Franciscan History, 1955

Hubbard, Margaret Ann, The Road to the King's Mountain, Doubleday & Co. Inc., 1963

Lyngheim, Linda, Father Junipero Serra, The

Traveling Missionary, Langtry Publications, 1986

Morgado, Martin J., Junipero Serra - A Pictorial Biography, Siempre Adelante Publishing, 1991

Repplier, Agnes, Junipero Serra, Pioneer Colonist of California, Doubleday & Co., 1933

About the author

Natalie Hernandez was born in Chicago, Illinois on March 28, 1929. She graduated from the University of Illinois and was married in Tokyo, Japan in 1953. After teaching school in California for 25 years she began writing historical novels for young people. She lives in Buellton, California with her husband who is also a retired teacher. They have 2 daughters and one son.